# NATURE WHIMSY

## A **WORDPLAY** COLORING BOOK

## Jessica Mazurkiewicz

Dover Publications, Inc.
Mineola, New York

Whimsical illustrations and descriptive words unite in this delightful coloring book geared toward advanced colorists and word enthusiasts. Thirty-one unique designs of plant and animal life include insects, flowers and leaves, birds, land and sea animals, and more. Pages are perforated and unbacked for easy removal from the book.

*Bibliographical Note*

*Nature Whimsy: A WordPlay Coloring Book* is a new work, first published by Dover Publications, Inc., in 2017.

*International Standard Book Number*

*ISBN-13: 978-0-486-81593-0*
*ISBN-10: 0-486-81593-5*

Manufactured in the United States by LSC Communications
81593501    2017
www.doverpublications.com

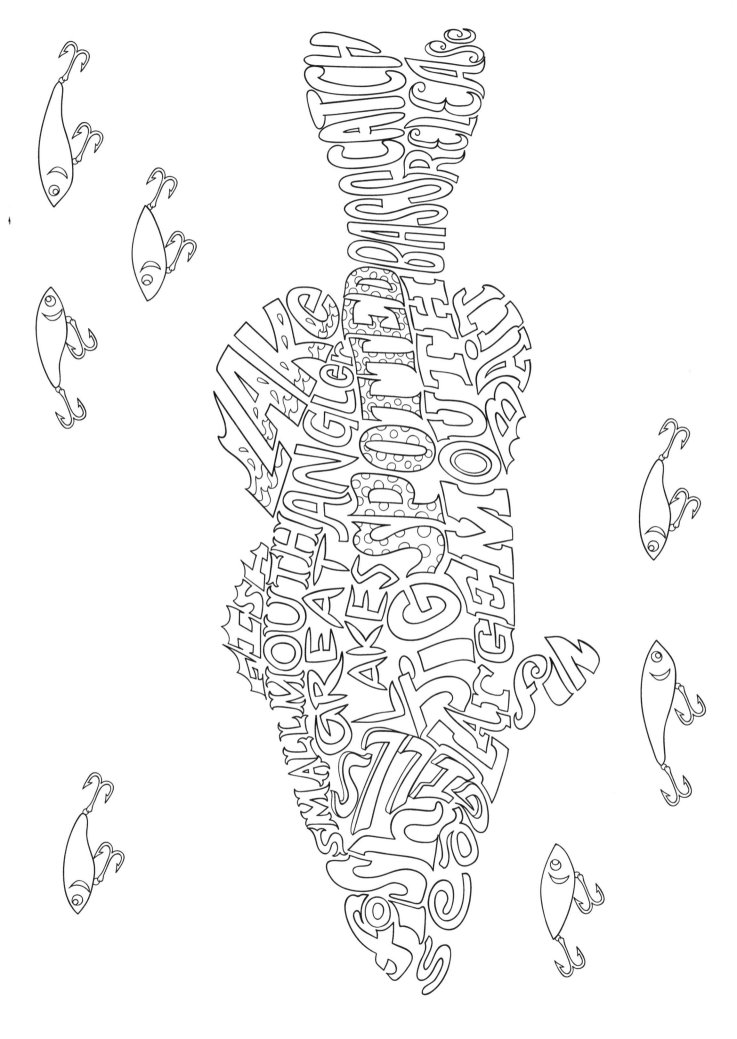